THE CATHARTIC TRUMP COLORING BOOK

Stress Relief For Frustrated Liberals

VOLUME 1

ILLUSTRATIONS BY
DAVID ZALESKI

"We had a crowd... I looked over that sea of people, and said to myself, 'wow.' And I've seen crowds before. Big, big crowds. That was some crowd."

- Donald Trump

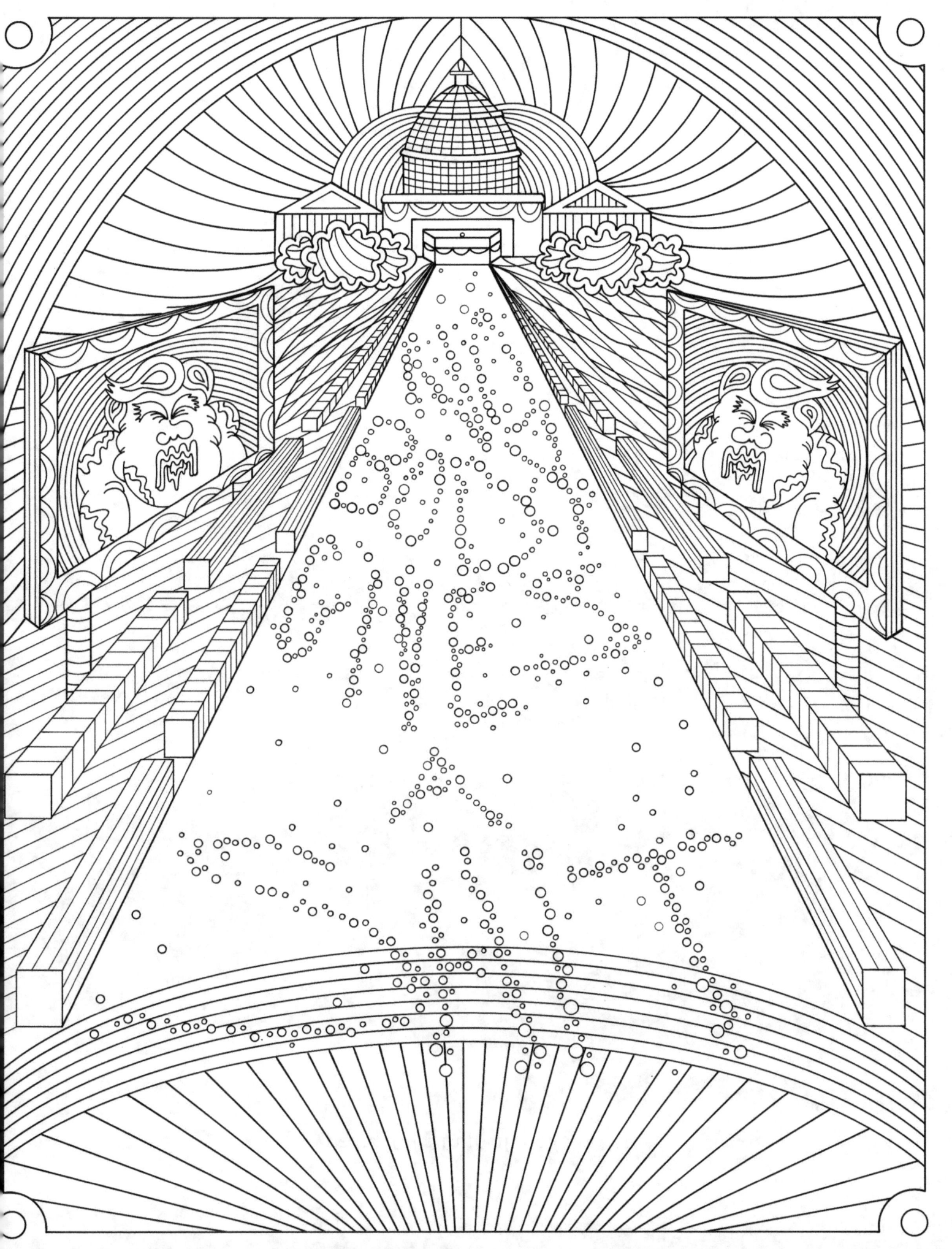

Page left blank for bleed

"I think I'd get along very well with Vladimir Putin, I just think so. People say 'what do you mean?'

I think I'd get along well with him."

- Donald Trump

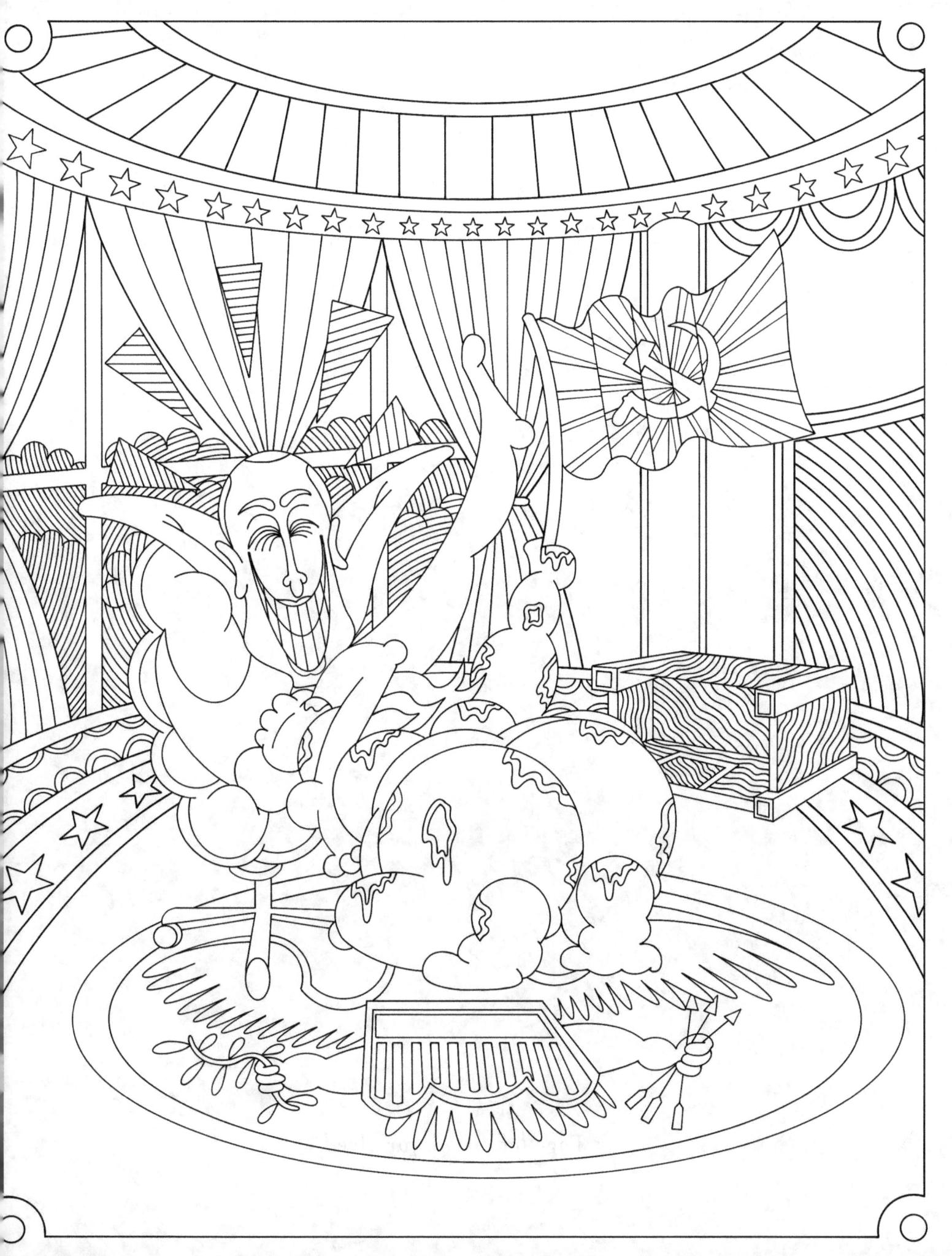

Page left blank for bleed

"Serious voter fraud... why isn't the media reporting on this? Serious bias - big problem!"

- Donald Trump

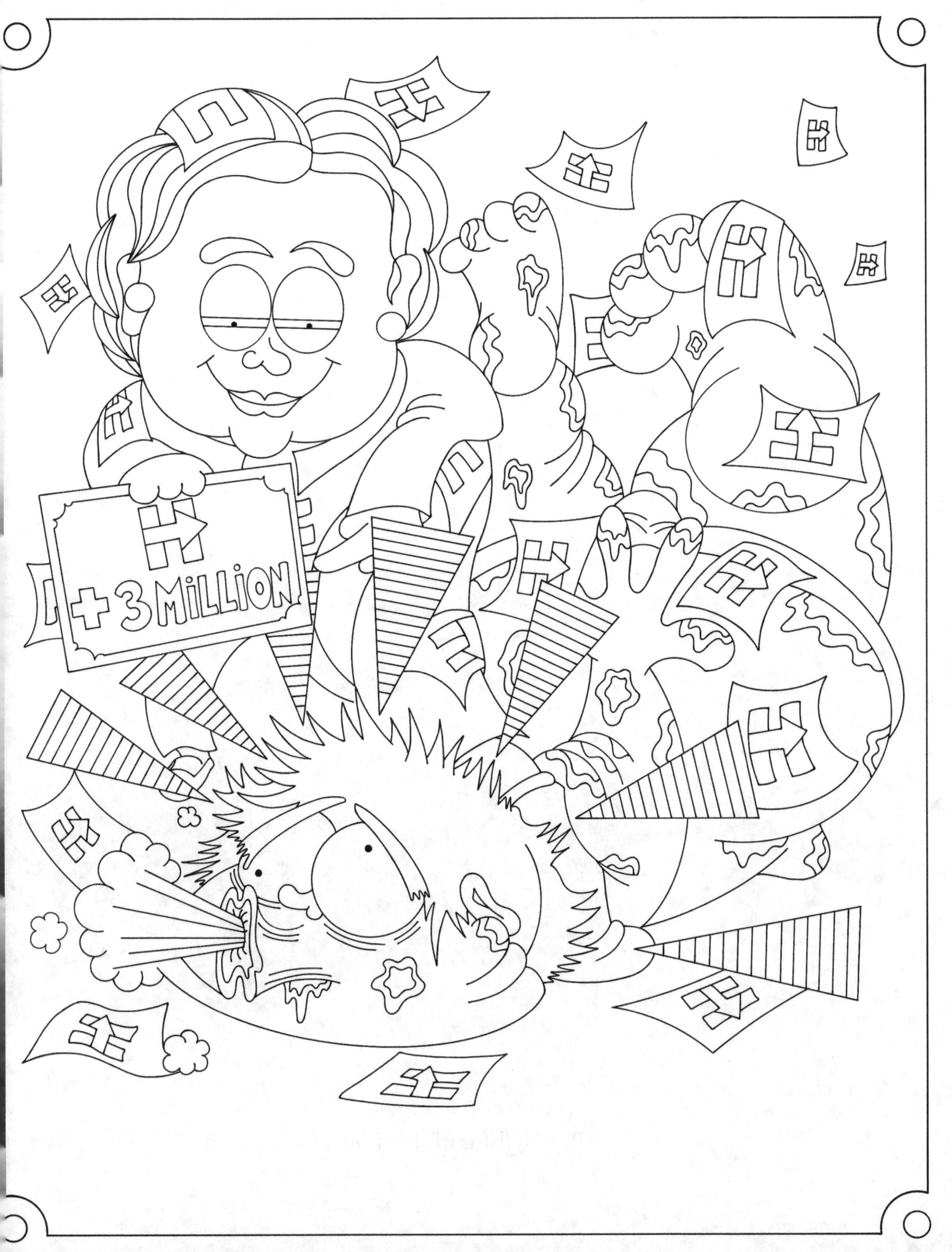

Page left blank for bleed

"You can get the baby out of here."

- Donald Trump

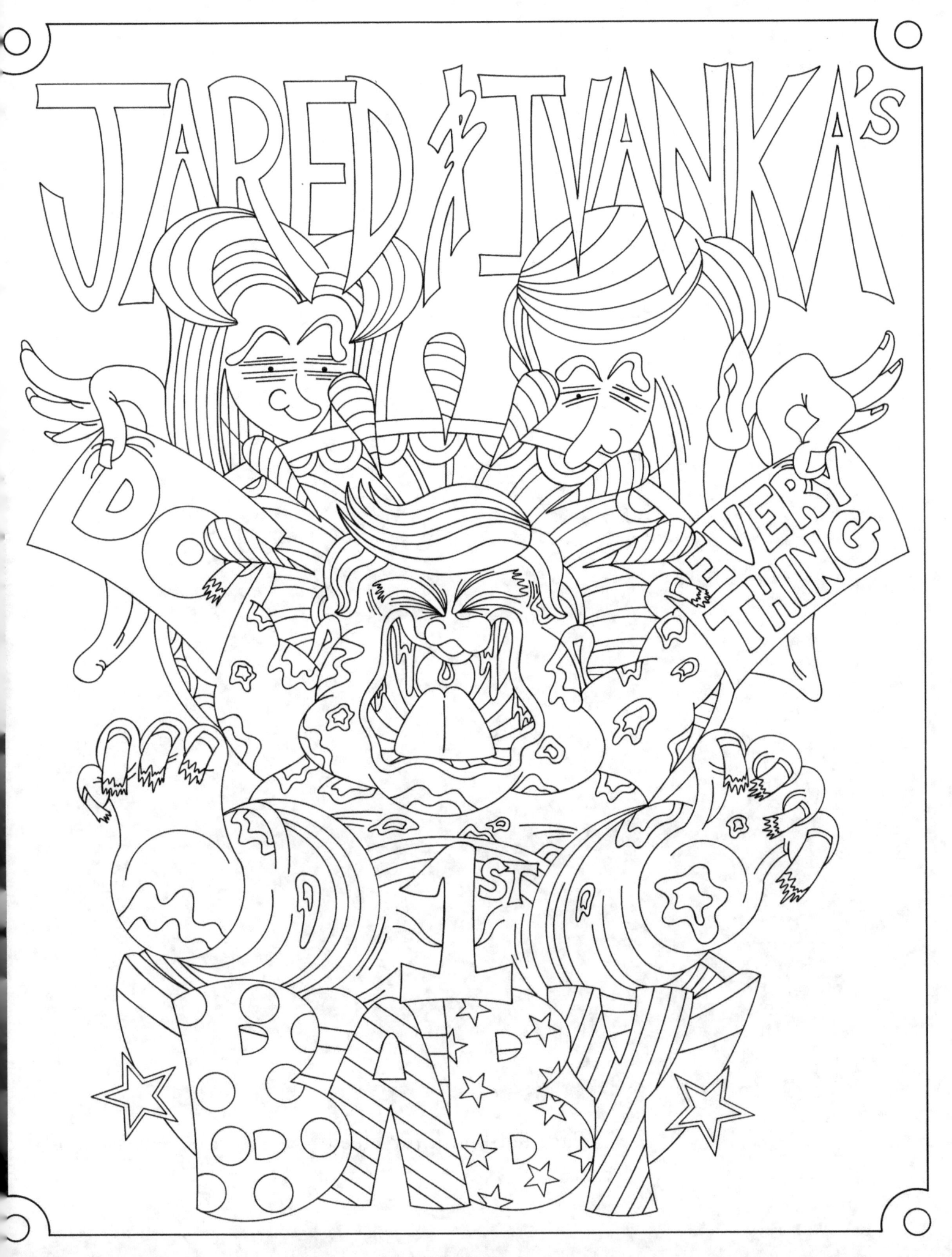

"Other people paint beautifully on canvas or write wonderful poetry. I like making deals, preferably big deals. That's how I get my kicks."

- Donald Trump

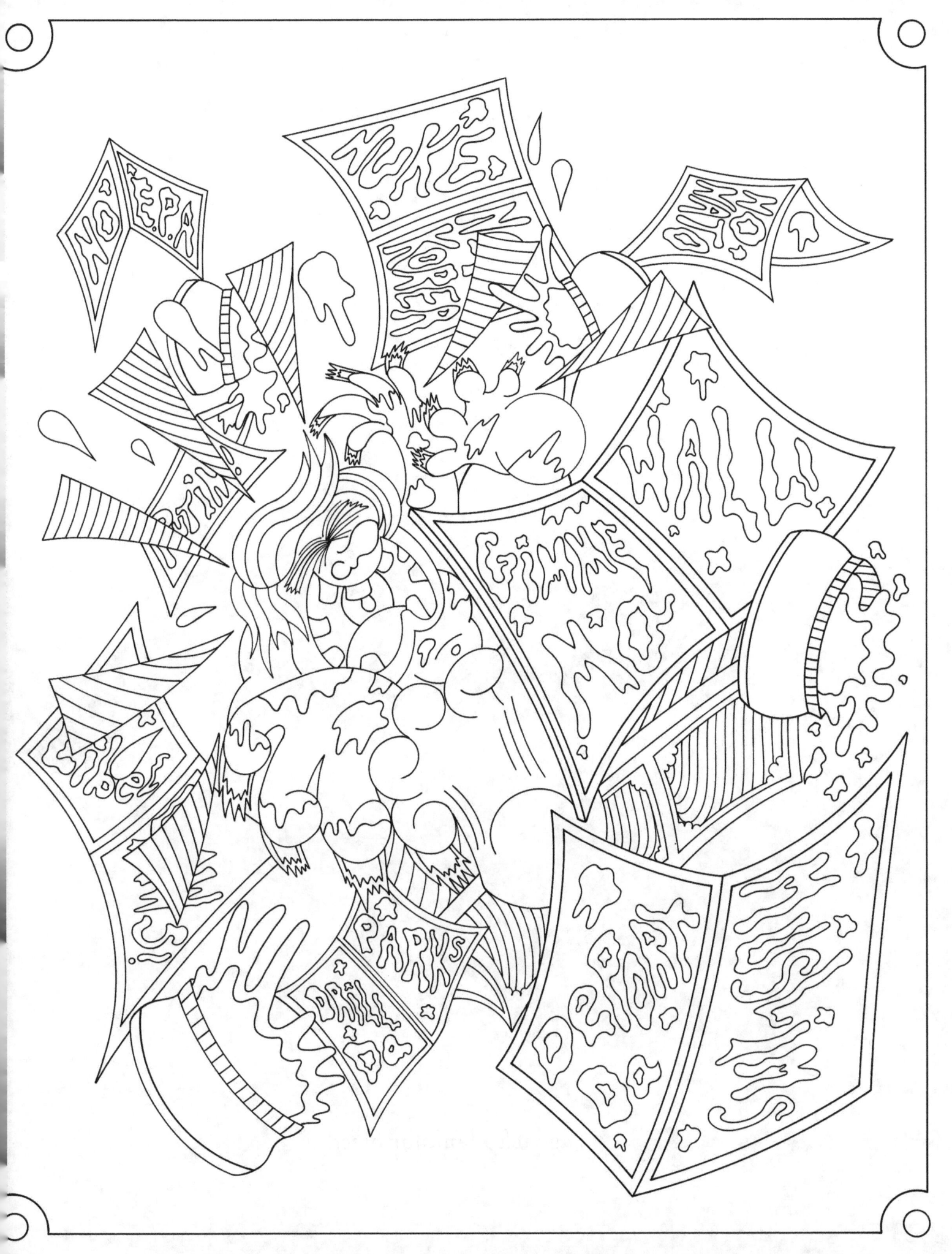

"Doing my best to disregard the many inflammatory President O statements and roadblocks. Thought it was going to be a smooth transition - NOT!"

- Donald Trump

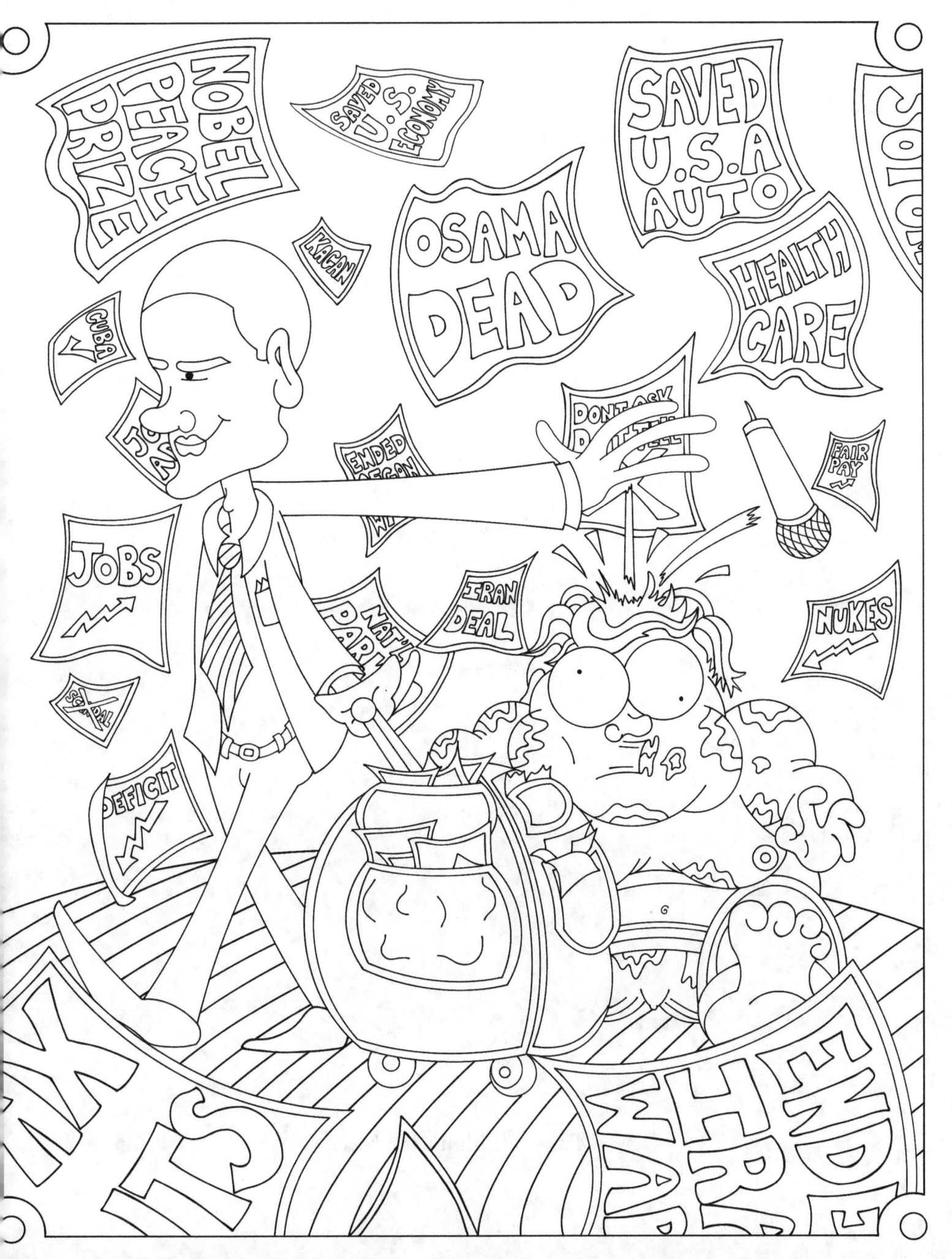

"I do not wear a toupee. It's my hair , I swear!"

- Donald Trump

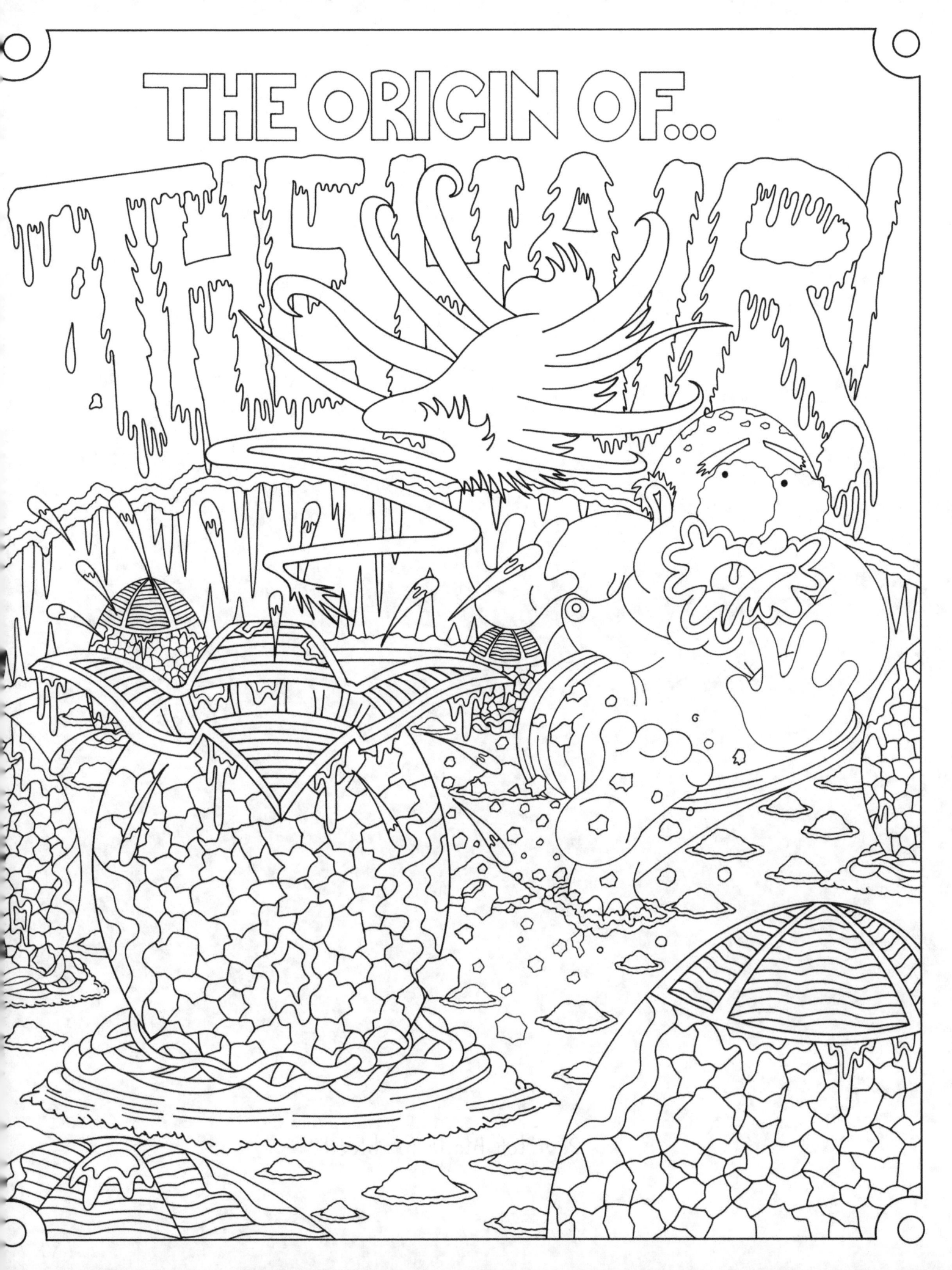

"He referred to my hands - 'if they're small, something else must be small.' I guarantee you there's no problem. I guarantee."

- Donald Trump

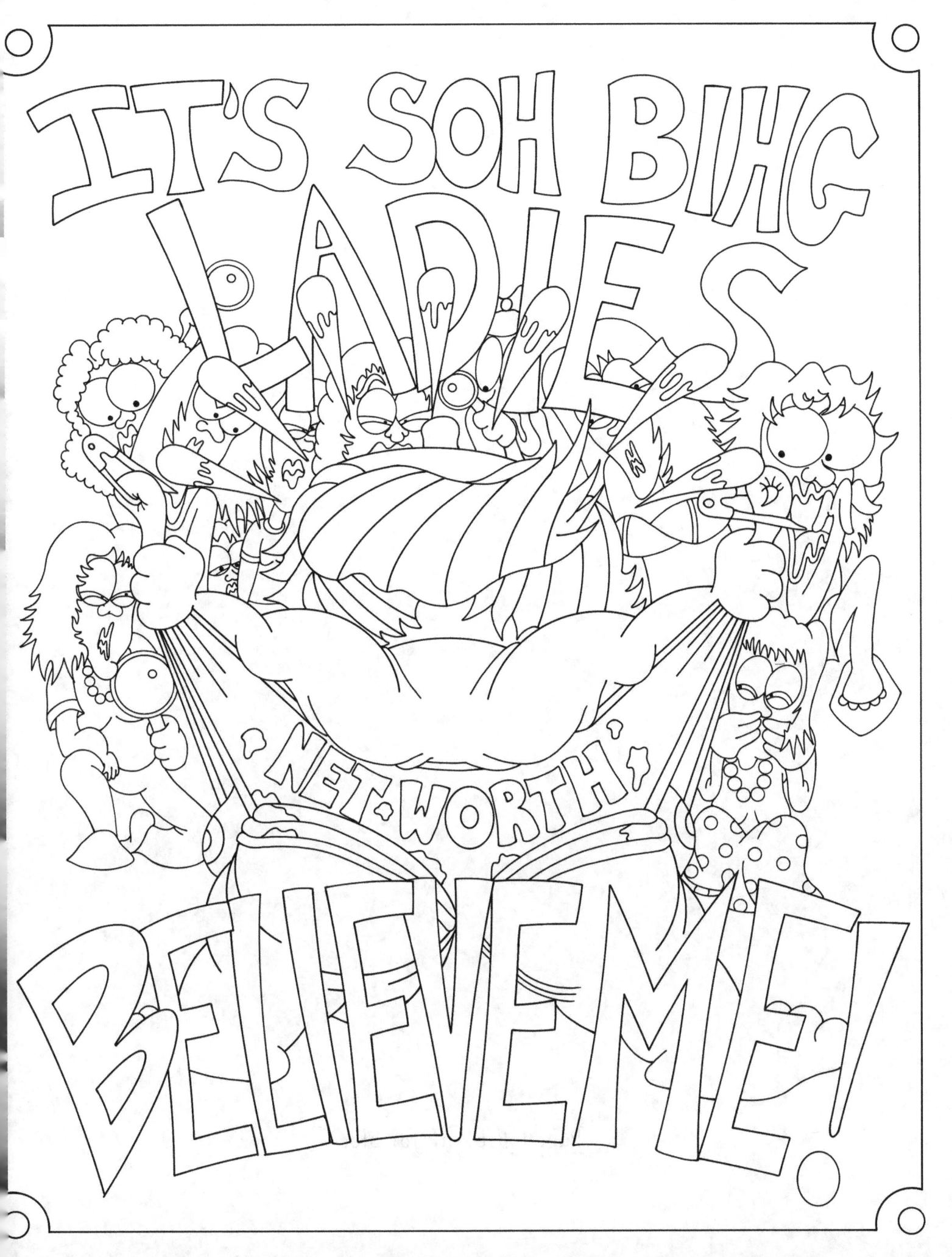

Page left blank for bleed

"My new game... I think you'll like it."

- Donald Trump

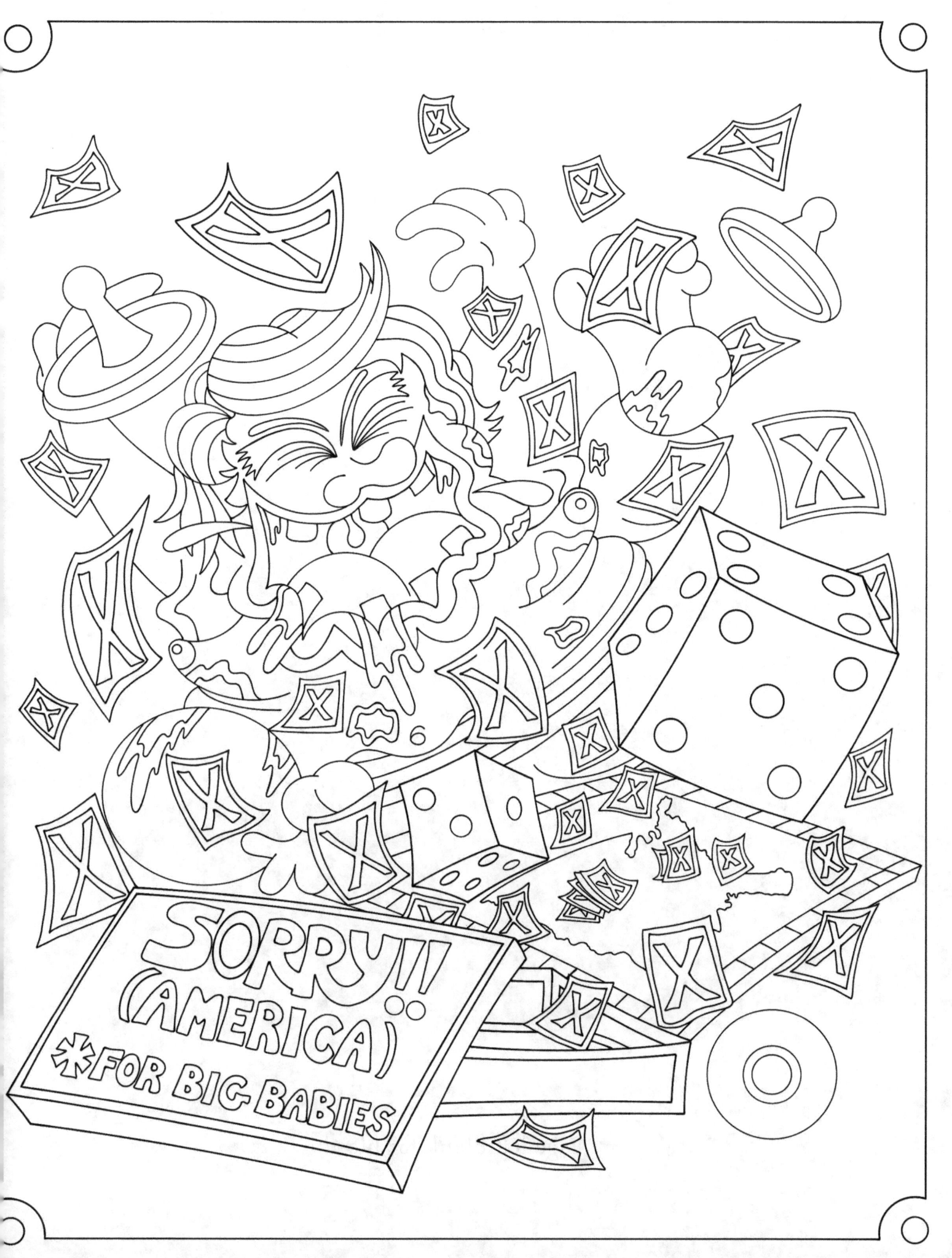

Page left blank for bleed

"Believe me. You're going to be
proud again to be miners."

- Donald Trump

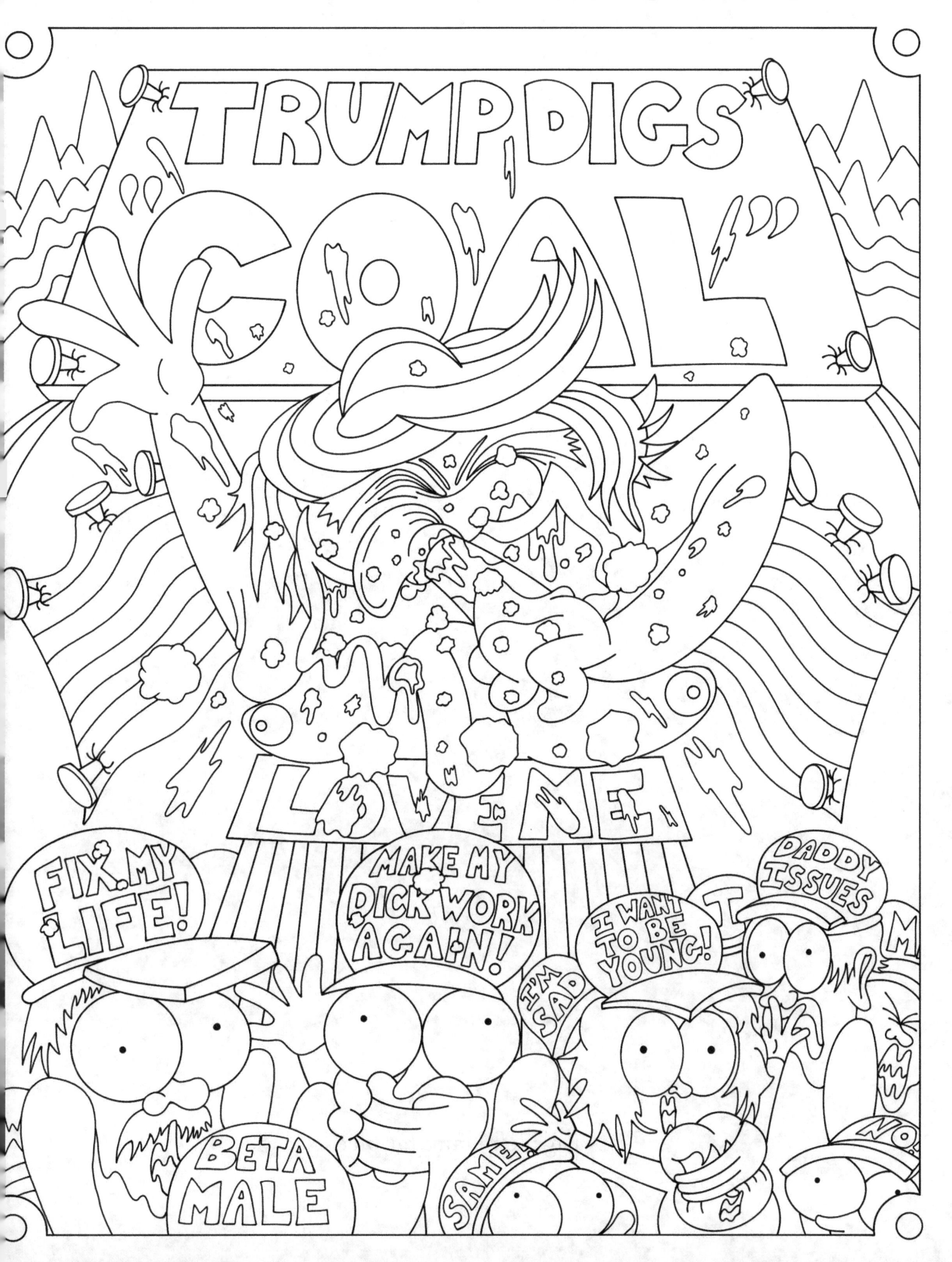

Page left blank for bleed

"My whole life is about winning. I don't lose often. I almost never lose."

- Donald Trump

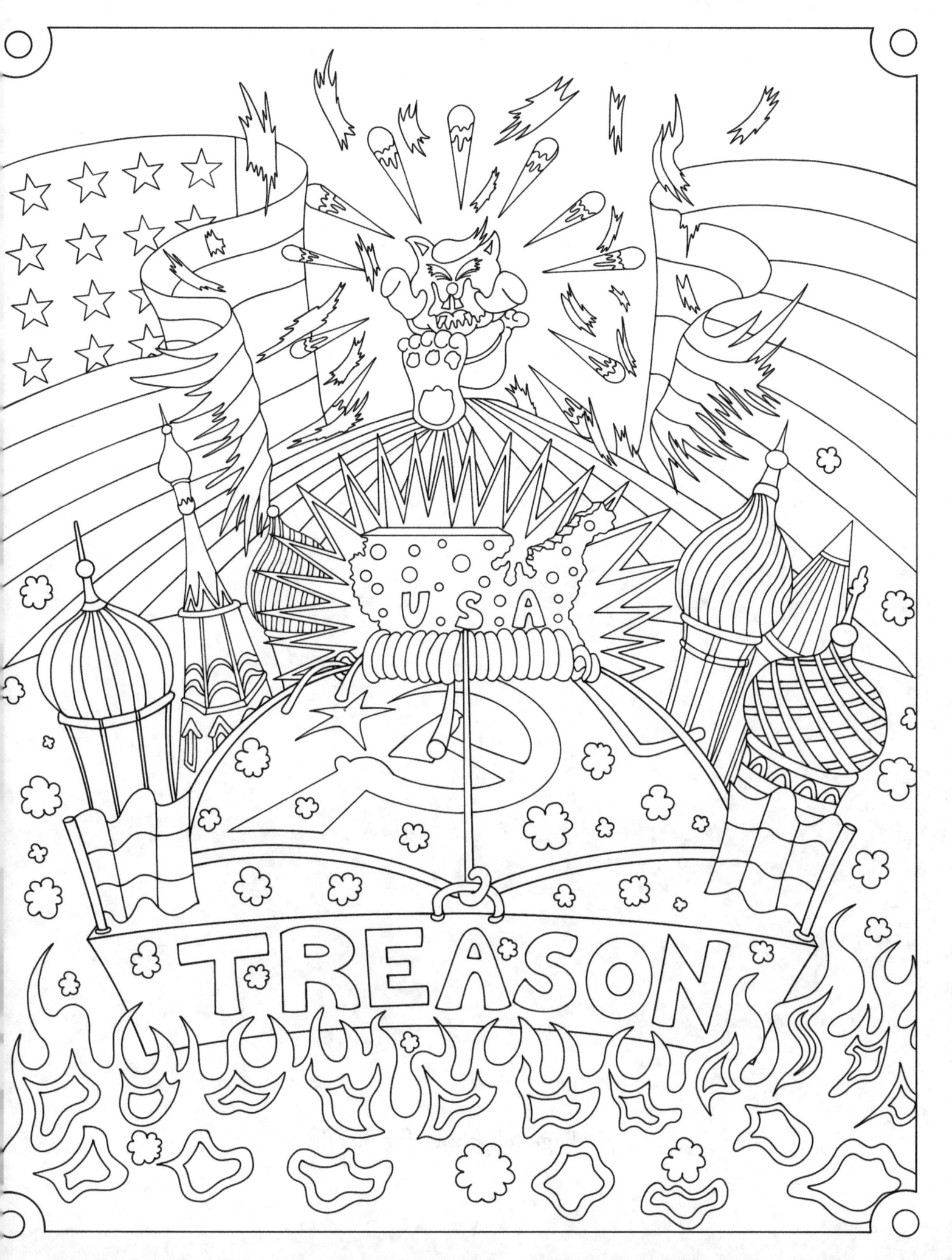

Page left blank for bleed

"FBI director said Crooked Hillary compromised our national security. No charges. Wow!"

- Donald Trump

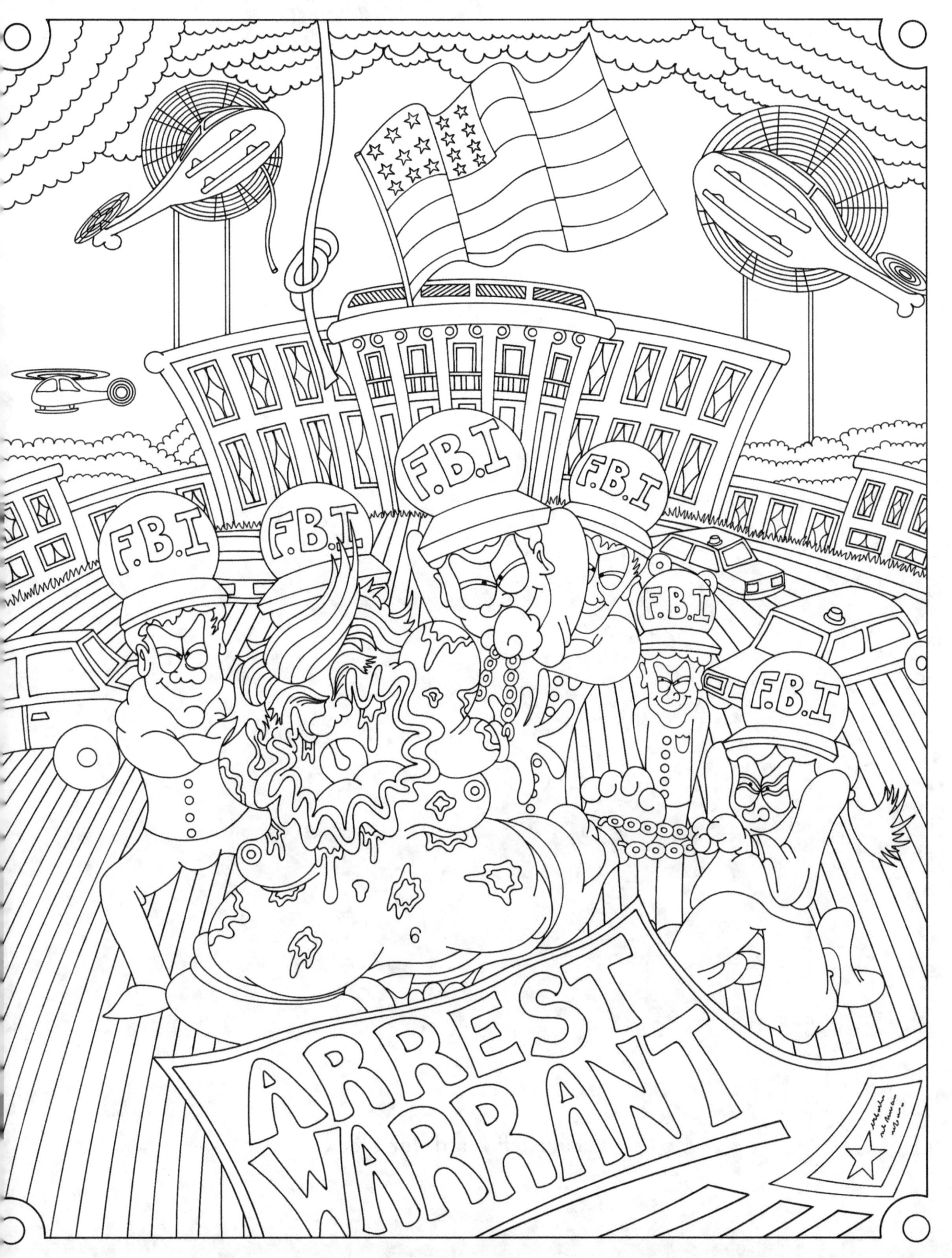

Page left blank for bleed

"No puppet! No puppet! You're the puppet!"

- Donald Trump

Page left blank for bleed

"Beautiful. Great plane... a very special plane for a lot of reasons."

- Donald Trump

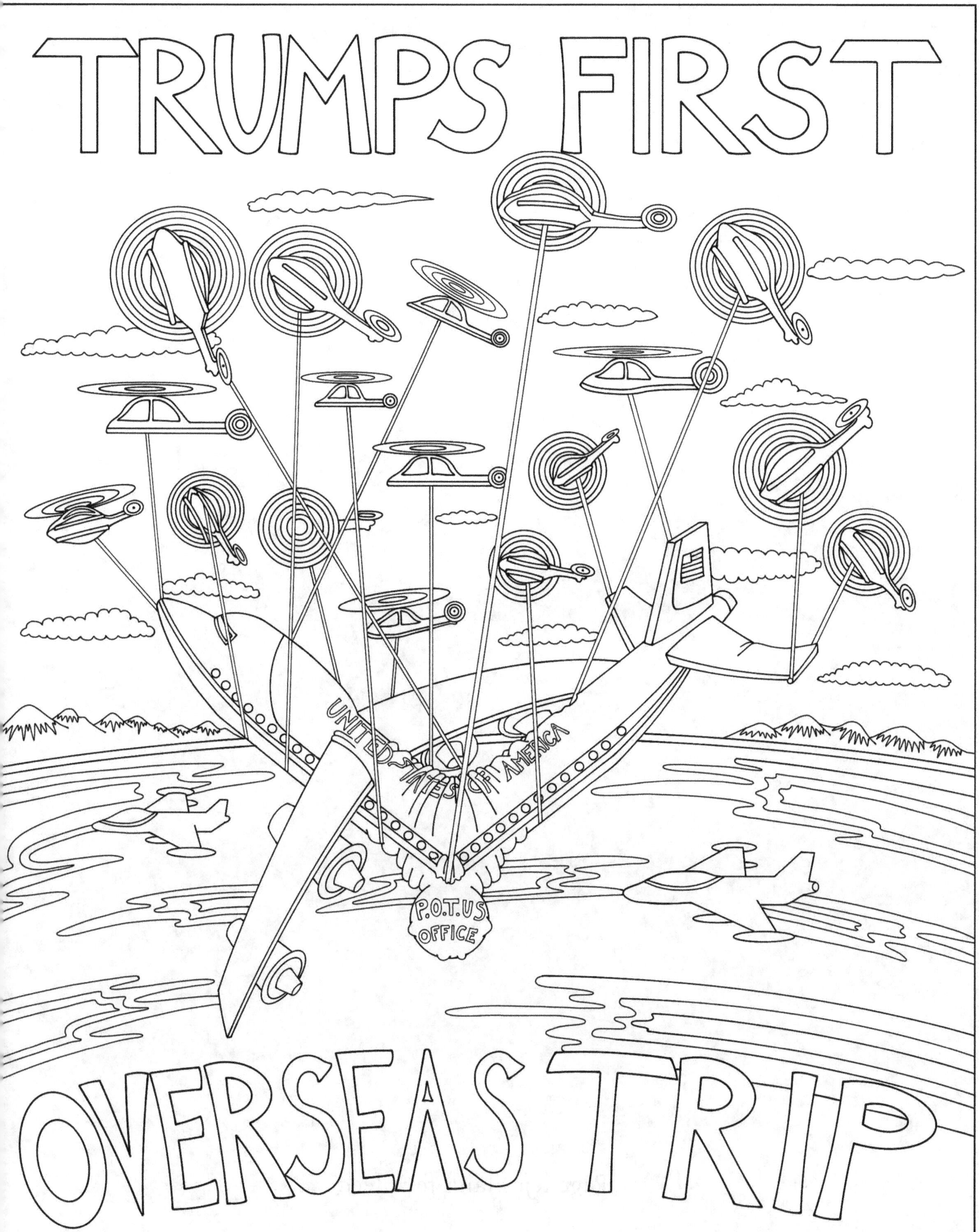
TRUMPS FIRST
UNITED STATES OF AMERICA
P.O.T.U.S OFFICE
OVERSEAS TRIP

Page left blank for bleed

"I inherited a mess!"

- Donald Trump

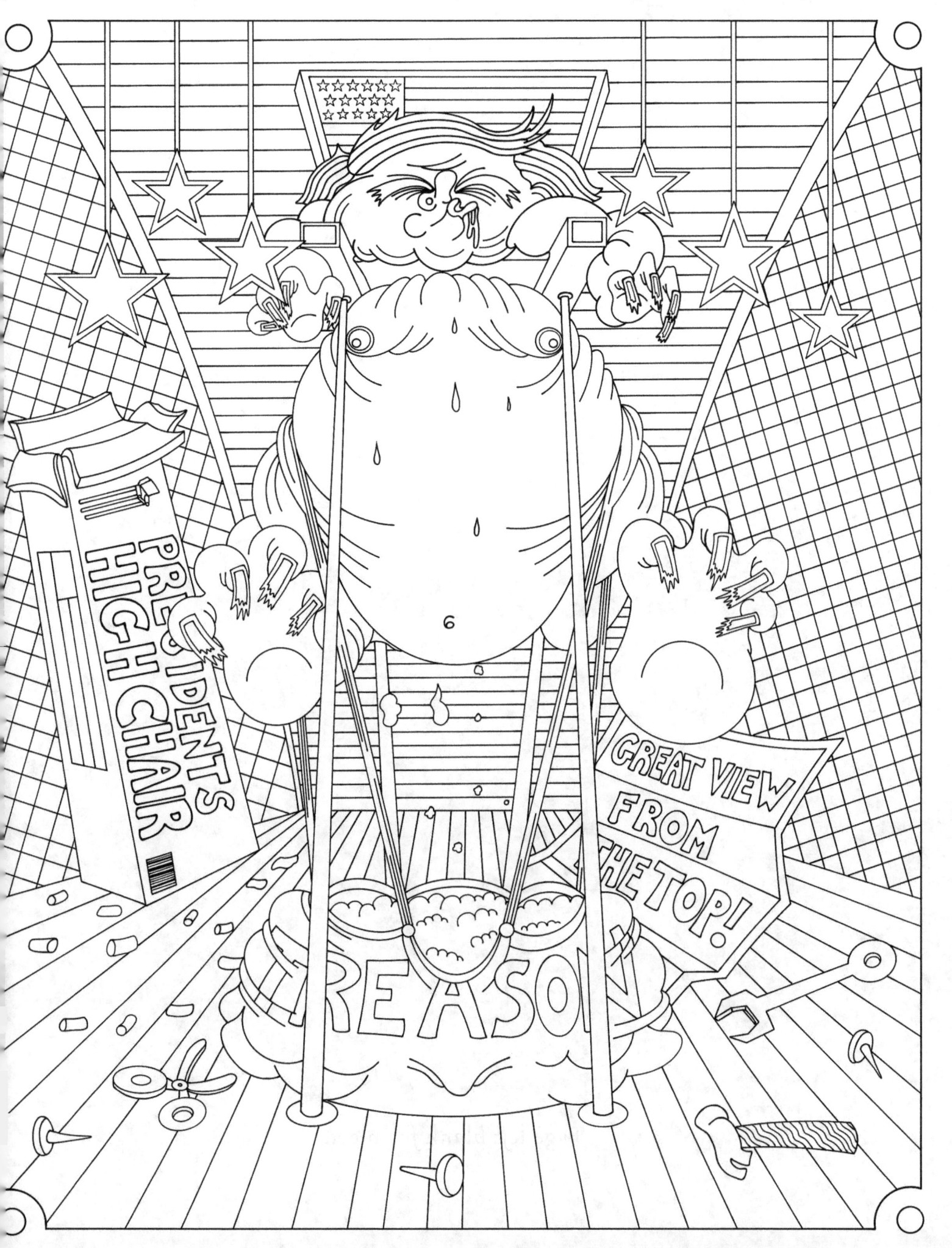

Page left blank for bleed

"This crime wave ends when Donald Trump becomes president. Believe me."

- Donald Trump

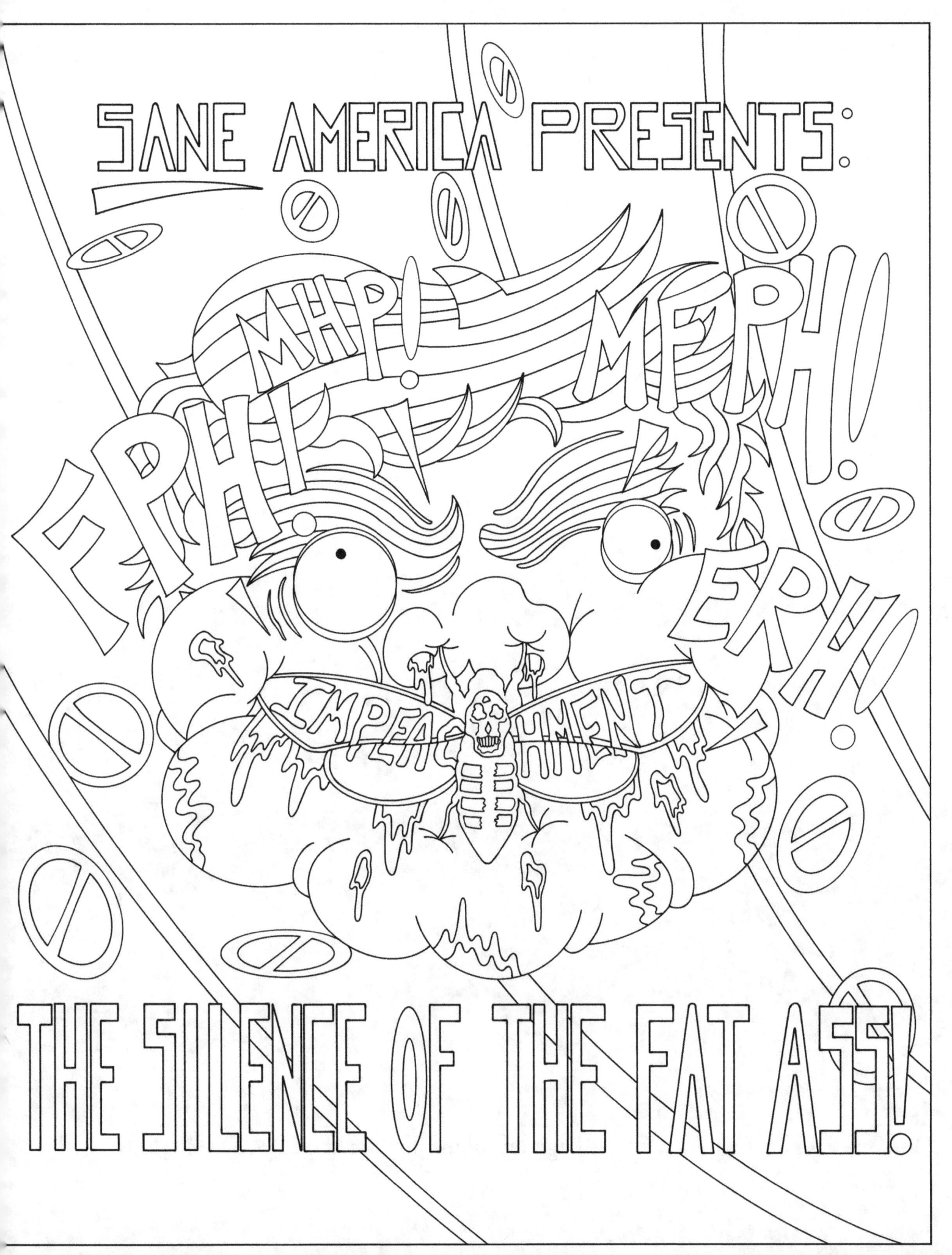

"I know Melania, I'm not going to be doing the diapers, I'm not going to be making the food... she'll be an unbelievable mother."

- Donald Trump

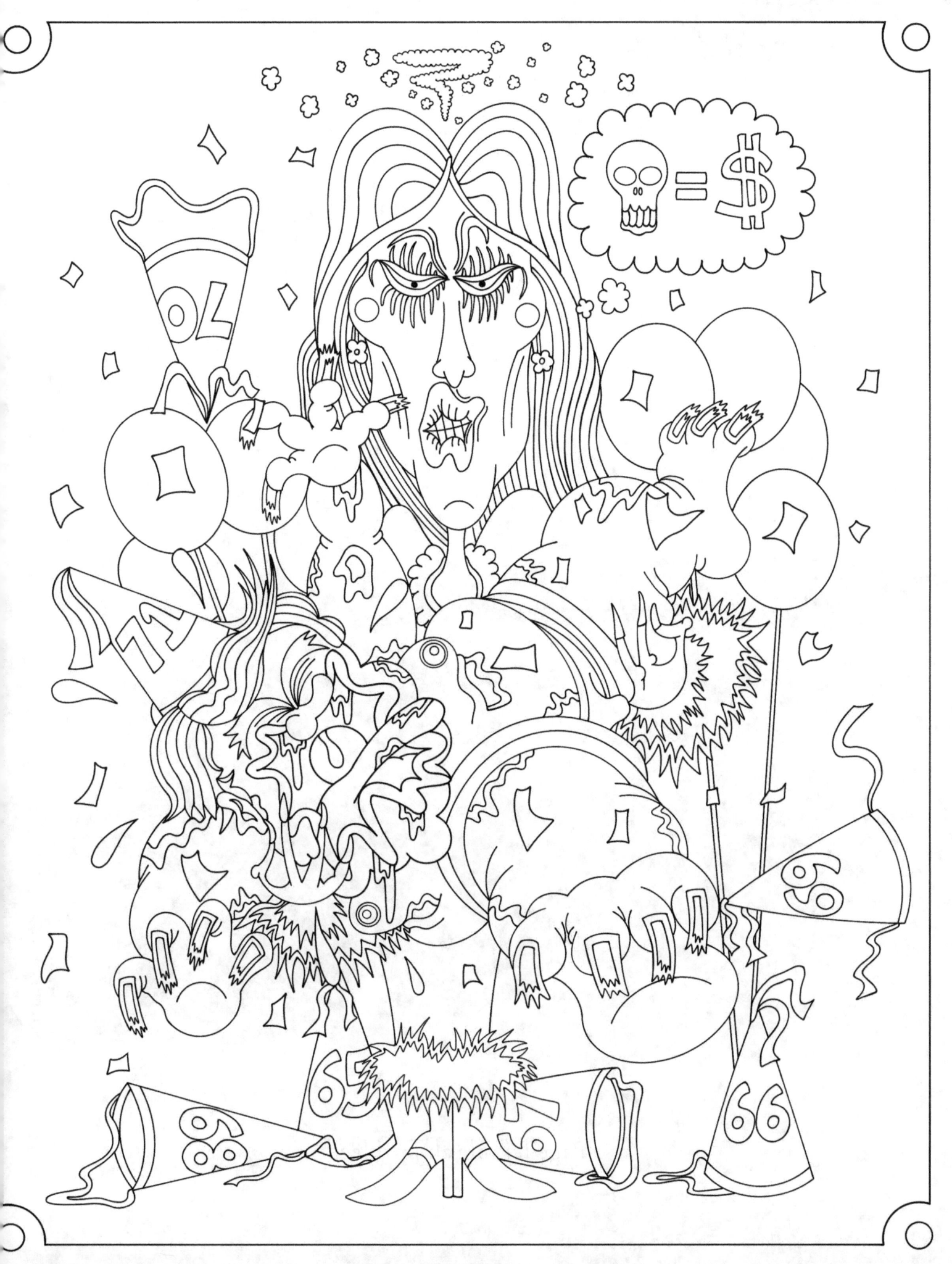

Page left blank for bleed

"Our vice president, I think I'm speaking for both... he has one hell of a good marriage going."

- Donald Trump

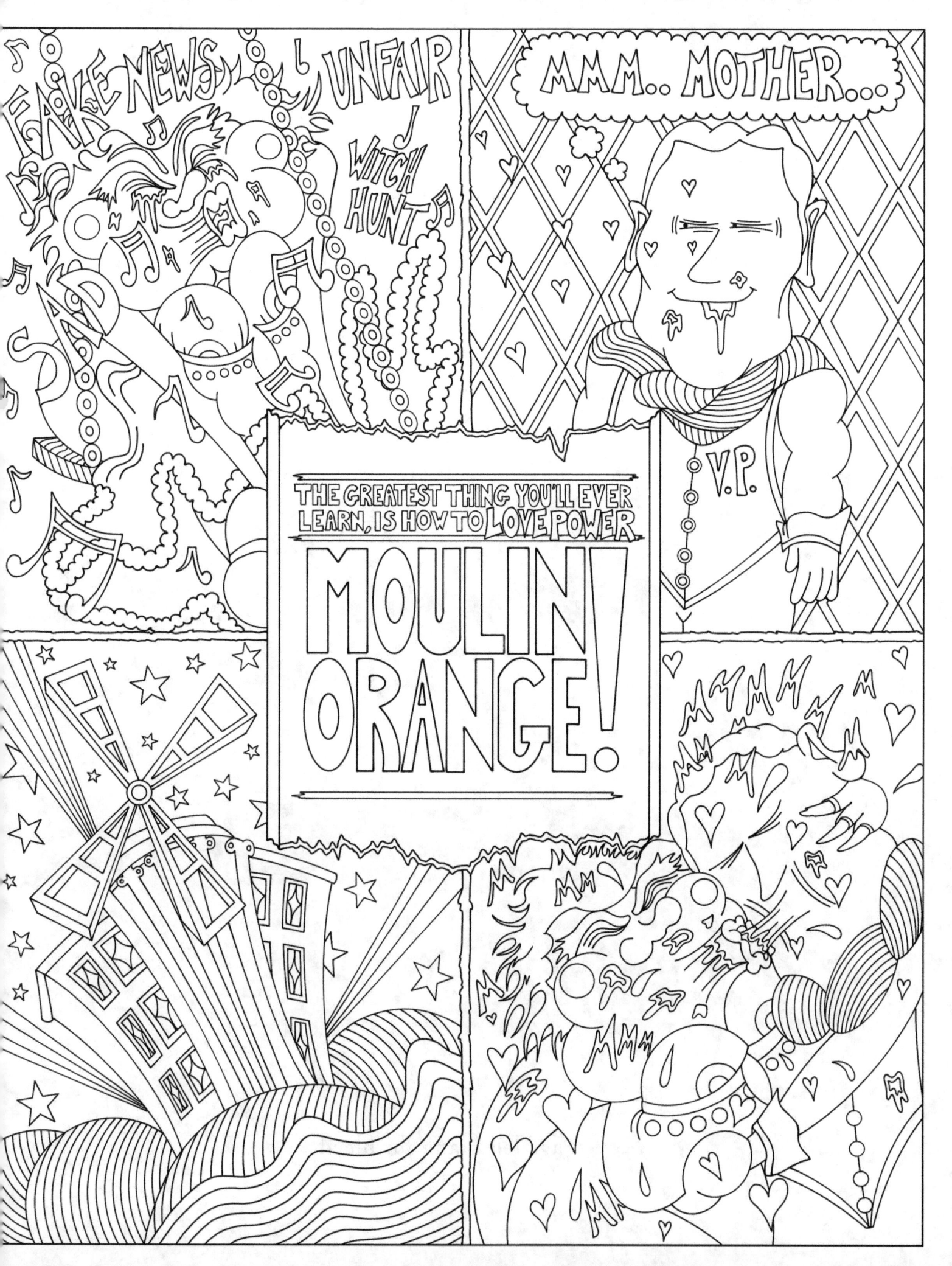

Page left blank for bleed

"I would call up those countries...
and say 'fellas, you haven't paid
for years. Give us the money or
get the hell out.' ...Maybe NATO
will disolve, and that's OK."

- Donald Trump

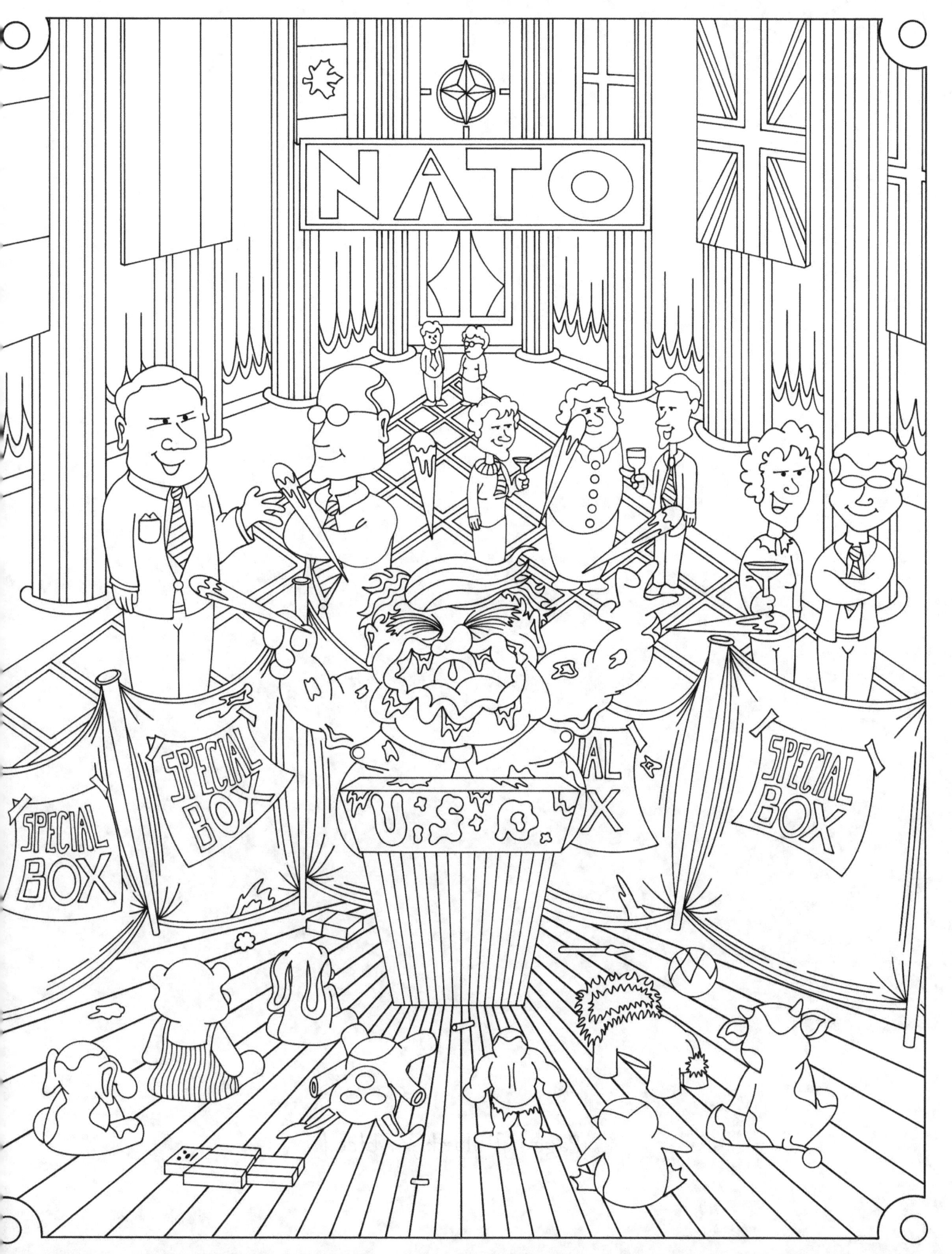

Page left blank for bleed

"This very expensive GLOBAL WARMING bullshit has got to stop."

- Donald Trump

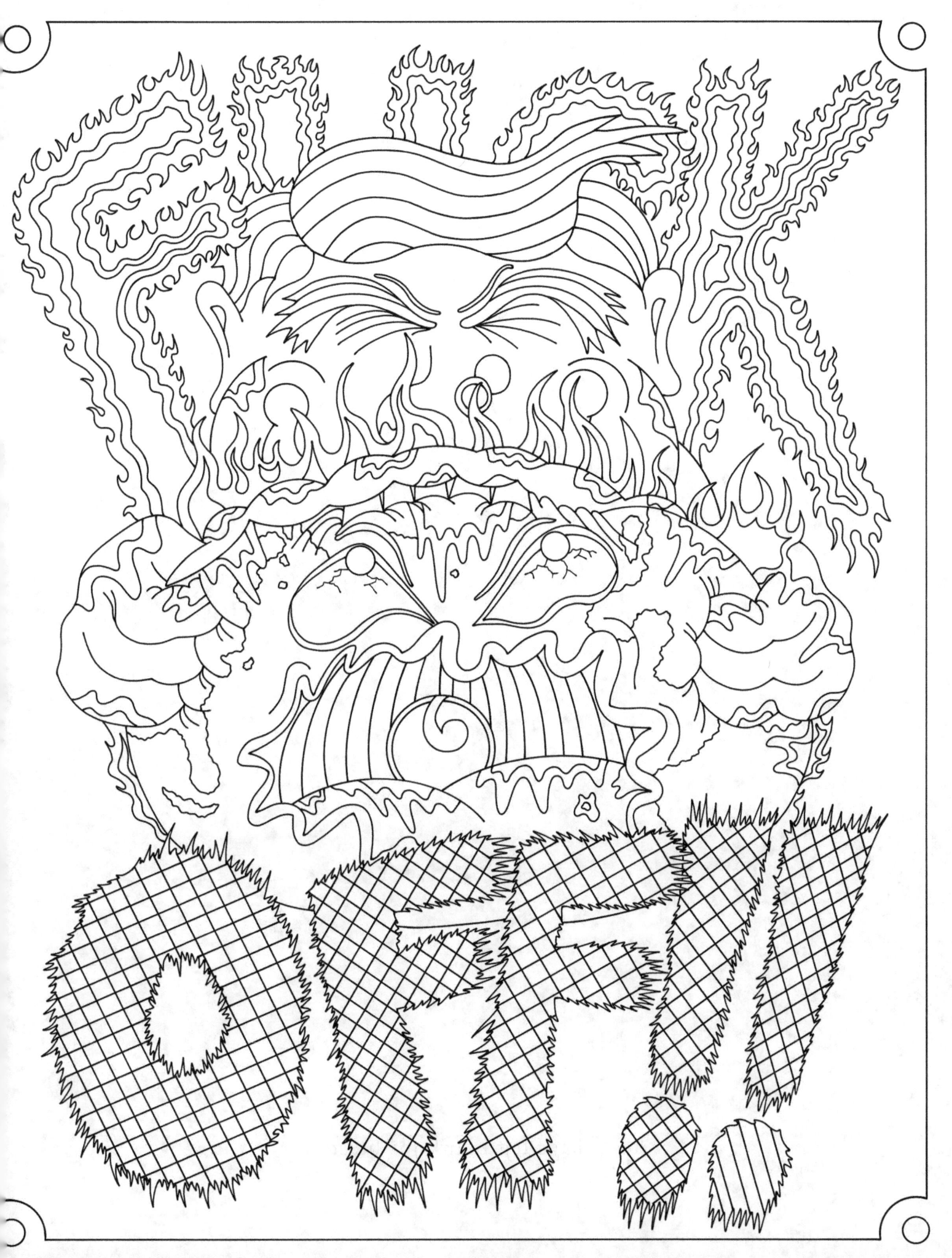

Page left blank for bleed

THE CATHARTIC TRUMP COLORING BOOK

Stress Relief For Frustrated Liberals

VOLUME 1

ILLUSTRATIONS BY
DAVID ZALESKI